WELCOME TO THE FUTURE, IT'S FINALLY HERE

By J. Poole

Forward

In a world brimming with technological marvels, where artificial intelligence and robotics redefine the boundaries of possibility, it's easy to feel overwhelmed by the rapid pace of change. Yet, amidst this whirlwind of innovation, there lies an opportunity to shape a future that aligns with our deepest values and aspirations.

This book invites you to explore the transformative potential of technologies like autonomous vehicles, humanoid robots, and advanced AI, not as distant concepts but as tangible forces shaping our present and future. It's an invitation to engage in thoughtful dialogue about the ethical considerations, societal impacts, and the very essence of what it means to be human in an age of intelligent machines.

Within these chapters, you'll encounter thought-provoking questions and insights that challenge conventional notions of work, urban planning, and economic models. You'll delve into the potential of an Age of Plenitude, where AI-driven automation could create a world of abundance, addressing fundamental human needs and fostering unprecedented levels of creativity and innovation.

But this journey isn't just about embracing technological marvels; it's about navigating the ethical dilemmas that accompany them. It's about ensuring that AI is developed and used responsibly, that automation benefits all members of society, and that human values remain at the forefront of our technological endeavors.

As you turn these pages, consider yourself an active participant in shaping the future. Engage with the ideas presented, challenge assumptions, and contribute to the ongoing conversation about how we can harness these transformative technologies for the betterment of humanity.

The future isn't something that happens to us; it's something we create. Let this book be your guide as you navigate the exciting possibilities and challenges that lie ahead, empowering you to make informed choices and contribute to a future where technology and humanity thrive in harmony.

Table of Contents

Chapter 1: The Autonomous Revolution

Self-Driving Cars and the Road Ahead

Imagine you're heading to a party in a sleek, futuristic vehicle. There's no driver, no steering wheel, and no need to worry about traffic. You're in a Tesla Cyber Cab, an autonomous car that navigates the roads with precision and ease. As you cruise along, you listen to your favorite music and enjoy the scenery passing by. This isn't a far-off dream; it's a reality that's unfolding right now.

Companies like Tesla and Waymo are developing autonomous vehicles that can drive themselves without human intervention. These cars use advanced sensors, cameras, and artificial intelligence to understand their surroundings and make real-time decisions. The goal is to create a transportation system that's not only more convenient but also significantly safer.

Safety First: Reducing Accidents on the Road

Human error is a leading cause of car accidents. According to the National Highway Traffic Safety Administration (NHTSA), approximately 94% of serious crashes are due to human error, including factors like distracted driving, speeding, and impaired driving. Autonomous vehicles have the potential to dramatically reduce these incidents.

Imagine a world where accidents are rare, where roads are safer for everyone—drivers, passengers, cyclists, and pedestrians alike. Studies suggest that self-driving cars could reduce traffic accidents by up to 90%. McKinsey & Company estimates that widespread adoption of autonomous vehicles could save thousands of lives each year in the United States alone.

Real-world testing data supports these optimistic projections.. Waymo's fully autonomous taxis are already on the streets of Phoenix, Arizona, providing rides to the public with no human drivers. This service marks a milestone in autonomous vehicle technology, demonstrating that the future of driverless transportation is not only possible but already in motion. As cities around the world prepare for wider adoption, we can expect autonomous vehicles to revolutionize urban travel, making commutes faster, safer, and more sustainable.

However, challenges remain. Autonomous vehicles must navigate complex environments and handle unexpected situations, known as "edge cases," such as unusual road debris or erratic behavior from other drivers. Adverse weather conditions like heavy rain or snow can impair sensors and cameras, affecting the vehicle's ability to navigate safely. Despite these hurdles, the potential benefits in reducing accidents and saving lives make pursuing autonomous vehicle technology a worthwhile endeavor.

Changing the Way We Travel

Autonomous vehicles could also transform our daily commutes and long-distance travel. With self-driving cars, you could use your travel time to relax, work, or spend time with family. Traffic congestion might decrease as cars communicate with each other to optimize routes and reduce bottlenecks. Imagine a seamless flow of traffic where vehicles adjust their speed and direction collaboratively to prevent jams.

Moreover, these vehicles are likely to be electric, contributing to a reduction in greenhouse gas emissions and helping combat climate change. Electric autonomous vehicles could lead to cleaner air in our cities and a smaller carbon footprint overall.

Economic and Social Implications

The shift to autonomous vehicles isn't just about technology; it's about redefining our relationship with transportation. Ride-sharing services using self-driving cars could become more affordable and convenient, reducing the need for personal car ownership. This could have significant economic implications, from reducing household expenses related to car ownership to reshaping industries like auto insurance and car manufacturing. However, it's essential to consider the impact on jobs. Professional drivers, such as truckers and taxi drivers, might face displacement.

Addressing these challenges requires proactive measures, like retraining programs and educational initiatives, to help affected workers transition into new roles in the evolving economy.

Reflection Questions

How do you envision autonomous vehicles changing your daily life in the

next decade?

What concerns do you have about the widespread adoption of self-driving cars, and how might society address them?

In what ways can we balance technological advancements with the potential impact on jobs in the transportation industry?

Chapter 2: Redesigning Our Cities

From Concrete Jungles to Community Spaces

Take a moment to think about all the space dedicated to parking lots and garages in your city. These areas occupy vast amounts of land that often sit empty or underused, especially with the rise of ride-sharing and public transportation options. As autonomous vehicles become more prevalent and reduce the need for personal car ownership, we could see a significant decrease in the demand for parking spaces.

A Realistic Transformation

While it's unlikely that all parking lots will disappear, repurposing 30–40% of existing parking areas is a realistic possibility. This shift presents an exciting opportunity to rethink how we use this valuable urban land. Imagine if a portion of these parking lots were transformed into spaces that benefit the community. Picture lush green parks where families picnic and children play, community gardens where residents grow fresh produce, or affordable housing units that help address the housing crisis in many cities. The land could also be used for community centers, libraries, or small businesses like local markets and artisan shops.

Transforming Urban Landscapes

Cities like Singapore and Barcelona are already leading the charge in integrating AI and IoT (Internet of Things), technologies into their infrastructure, creating smarter, more efficient urban environments. In Singapore, smart traffic management systems use real-time data to reduce congestion, while AI-powered energy grids optimize electricity usage across the city. Similarly, Barcelona has implemented sensors throughout the city to monitor air quality, noise levels, and waste management, improving sustainability and public health. These early examples of smart city initiatives showcase how AI can not only optimize resources but also enhance the quality of life for urban residents, providing a blueprint for the cities of tomorrow. In cities around the world, initiatives are already underway to repurpose underutilized spaces:

Seattle, USA: The city has programs to convert underused parking lots into affordable housing complexes, integrating retail spaces on the ground floor to create vibrant, mixed-use neighborhoods.

Melbourne, Australia: Some parking areas are being transformed into parks with playgrounds and recreational facilities, enhancing the quality of life for residents.

Copenhagen, Denmark: Known for its sustainable urban planning,

Copenhagen is repurposing parking spaces to expand bike lanes and pedestrian zones, promoting healthier and more eco-friendly transportation options.

By thoughtfully repurposing a significant portion of parking lots, cities can create more livable, sustainable, and inclusive environments. This transformation isn't just about changing physical spaces; it's about reimagining how we live together and use shared resources for the greater good.

Environmental Benefits

Reducing the number of parking lots and increasing green spaces can lead to several environmental advantages:

Improved Air Quality: Plants and trees absorb carbon dioxide and release oxygen, helping to clean the air and reduce pollution.

Urban Heat Island Mitigation: Replacing asphalt with greenery lowers temperatures in cities, as plants absorb less heat than concrete surfaces.

Stormwater Management: Green spaces can absorb rainwater, reducing runoff and the risk of flooding during heavy rains.

Enhancing Community Well-being

Transforming parking lots into community-oriented spaces can have positive social impacts:

Strengthening Social Connections: Parks, community centers, and markets provide places for people to gather, fostering a sense of community and belonging.

Promoting Healthy Lifestyles: Access to recreational facilities and green spaces encourages physical activity and outdoor enjoyment.

Cultural Enrichment: Cultural centers and public art installations can celebrate local heritage and creativity, enriching the community's cultural landscape.

Challenges and Considerations

While the potential benefits are significant, there are challenges to consider:

Infrastructure Adaptation: Modifying existing parking structures requires investment and careful planning to ensure safety and functionality.

Balancing Needs: Cities must balance the needs of drivers who still require parking with the desire to repurpose spaces for other uses.

Community Involvement: Engaging local residents in the planning process is crucial to ensure that new developments meet the community's needs and desires.

The Role of Autonomous Vehicles

Autonomous vehicles play a key role in making this transformation possible. With convenient and affordable self-driving ride-sharing services, fewer people may feel the need to own personal vehicles. Self-driving cars can drop passengers off and continue to the next destination without needing to park nearby, reducing the demand for parking spaces in prime locations. Additionally, autonomous vehicles can communicate with each other to improve traffic efficiency, potentially allowing for narrower roads and more space for pedestrians and cyclists.

Looking Ahead

By reimagining how we use urban spaces, we can create cities that prioritize people over cars, enhancing quality of life and fostering stronger communities. This vision requires collaboration between city planners, governments, businesses, and residents. As we move towards this future, let's work together to ensure that the transformation of our cities leads to positive outcomes for everyone.

Reflection Questions

In what ways could your own community benefit from repurposing parking lots or underutilized spaces?

What challenges might your city face in attempting to transform these spaces, and how could they be addressed?

How can individuals get involved in urban planning decisions that affect their neighborhoods?

Chapter 3: The Rise of the Robots

Meet the Humanoid Robots Shaping Our Future

Imagine coming home from school or work to find that the house is clean, dinner is ready, and help with your homework is just a conversation away. But instead of a family member handling these tasks, it's a humanoid robot—a new class of machines designed to interact with the world the way we do. While Tesla's Optimus is one example, a whole landscape of humanoid robots is being developed by companies around the world. These robots are poised to revolutionize industries, assist in daily tasks, and change the way we think about work and automation.

A New Generation of Humanoid Robots

Humanoid robots are designed with a human-like form, enabling them to operate in environments built for people. They can navigate spaces, use tools, and perform tasks much like we do. Let's explore some of the leading projects shaping the future of robotics.

Tesla's Optimus Robot

Tesla has made significant strides in humanoid robotics with their Optimus project. Designed to assist with general-purpose tasks in factories and homes, Optimus aims to relieve humans from labor-intensive or repetitive tasks, using its human-like form to operate in environments built for people. While still in development, Tesla envisions a future where Optimus is mass-produced and integrated into daily life—helping with everything from household chores to complex industrial tasks, showcasing the true potential of humanoid robots to revolutionize industries and daily living. With pricing expected to be less than a new car they aim to provide Optimus to more than just the financially well off with a goal to have one in every home.

Agility Robotics' Digit

Based in the United States, Agility Robotics has developed *Digit*, a bipedal robot engineered for real-world applications. Standing about human height and equipped with arms and legs, Digit can navigate complex environments and perform tasks like package delivery and warehouse logistics.

Digit is already being tested in pilot programs, including partnerships with major companies like Amazon. By handling repetitive and physically demanding tasks, it reduces the strain on human workers and addresses labor shortages in industries like logistics and warehousing.

What sets Digit apart is its advanced mobility. Its design enables it to walk naturally, climb stairs, and navigate obstacles with ease, making it versatile for various industries. By integrating seamlessly into environments built for humans, Digit represents a significant step forward in the collaboration between humans and robots in the workplace.

Aptronic's Apollo

Aptronic has introduced *Apollo*, a general-purpose humanoid robot designed to work in real-world environments. Standing 5'8" tall and weighing 160 pounds, Apollo can carry a payload of up to 55 pounds. It features hot-swappable battery packs, each providing about four hours of runtime, allowing for continuous operation with simple battery changes.

Apollo's modular design allows it to be mounted on different mobility platforms, from stationary bases to mobile legs. Equipped with advanced software, Apollo enables point-and-click control, making it easy to develop and integrate into warehouse and manufacturing operations.

Aptronic has entered into a commercial agreement with Mercedes-Benz to pilot Apollo in manufacturing facilities. The robot will be used to automate physically demanding and repetitive tasks, such as bringing parts to the production line and delivering kits of parts later in the manufacturing process. This partnership represents a significant step in the deployment of humanoid robots in industrial settings.

Figure AI's Figure 01

Figure AI is developing *Figure 01*, a humanoid robot aimed at addressing labor shortages by undertaking labor-intensive or unsafe tasks. Capable of carrying up to 44 pounds and operating for up to five hours on a single charge, Figure 01 is designed to autonomously navigate complex environments and learn from its surroundings.

The company has made rapid progress, moving from initial renderings to unveiling a prototype capable of dynamic walking in less than a year. Figure AI has secured significant funding and strategic partnerships with companies like OpenAI and Microsoft to enhance the robot's AI capabilities. Figure 01 is intended for initial deployment in industries like manufacturing, logistics, warehousing, and retail. In the long term, the company envisions its humanoids assisting in homes, caring for the elderly, and potentially even being used in space expeditions.

Unitree Robotics' H1

Unitree Robotics has developed the *H1*, a powerful and agile humanoid robot known for its exceptional performance capabilities. Standing approximately 180 cm tall and weighing around 47 kg, the H1 is capable of running at speeds over 3 meters per second and performing complex movements like backflips—a remarkable achievement without the use of hydraulics.

The H1 features high-torque electric joint motors, each offering a peak torque of 360 Newton-meters. This advanced design showcases the potential for electric motors to achieve high performance in tasks traditionally thought to require hydraulic systems.

Prized for its affordability, with some models starting at just 16,000.00 U.S., the H1 aims to be a cost-effective option for businesses looking to integrate robotics into their operations. Its capabilities make it suitable for applications in logistics, manufacturing, and other sectors where agility and speed are essential.

Sanctuary AI's Phoenix

Phoenix is a humanoid robot developed by Sanctuary AI, designed to perform a wide range of tasks powered by an advanced AI control system called Carbon. Standing around 5'7" tall and weighing approximately 155 pounds, Phoenix is built to mimic human form and function.

One of Phoenix's standout features is its industry-leading robotic hands with 20 degrees of freedom, providing dexterity comparable to human hands. The Carbon system enables Phoenix to think and act to complete tasks like a person, using deep learning and reinforcement learning.

Sanctuary AI has begun commercial deployments, marking a significant milestone in the company's progress toward full commercialization. Phoenix is capable of performing hundreds of tasks across various industries, including healthcare, hospitality, logistics, retail, and warehousing.

Fourier Intelligence's GR-1

Fourier Intelligence has introduced the *GR-1*, a humanoid robot leveraging their expertise in rehabilitation technologies. Standing at 5'5" and weighing 121 pounds, the GR-1 can carry up to 110 pounds and features 44 degrees of freedom for human-like motion.

The robot's hands have 11 degrees of freedom, allowing it to securely grasp items and perform tasks with precision. The GR-1 is particularly focused on assisting in caregiving and physical therapy, addressing challenges posed by aging populations and labor shortages in healthcare.

The Impact of Humanoid Robots on Society

The development of these humanoid robots signifies a shift toward automation in various industries. They have the potential to transform the workforce by addressing labor shortages and taking on tasks that are labor-intensive, repetitive, or dangerous. While robots may displace certain jobs, they also create new opportunities in robot maintenance, programming, and supervision.

Humanoid robots are designed to work alongside humans, enhancing productivity and efficiency. In daily life, they could handle household chores, freeing up time for people to focus on personal interests and family. In healthcare, humanoid robots can assist with patient care, lifting, and rehabilitation exercises.

Ethical and Social Considerations

As robots become more integrated into our lives, several ethical and social considerations arise:

Safety and Accountability: Ensuring the safe operation of robots and establishing accountability in case of malfunctions is crucial. Clear guidelines and laws are needed to address liability issues.

Human Interaction: Maintaining human connections and avoiding over-reliance on robots for social needs is important for societal well-being. While robots can assist with tasks, they should not replace human relationships.

Access and Equality: Making sure that the benefits of robotic technology are accessible to all segments of society can help prevent widening social inequalities. This includes addressing cost barriers and ensuring that technology is designed with inclusivity in mind.

Challenges Ahead

While the advancements are exciting, several challenges need to be addressed:

Technical Limitations: Navigating complex, unstructured environments remains a significant hurdle for robots. Continuous development and innovation are required to improve their capabilities.

Regulatory Frameworks: Establishing laws and guidelines for the deployment and use of humanoid robots is essential to ensure safety, privacy, and ethical use.

Public Perception: Gaining public trust and acceptance of robots in daily life requires transparency and education about their capabilities and limitations. Addressing fears and misconceptions is important for smooth integration.

Looking to the Future

The rise of humanoid robots represents a significant milestone in technological advancement. Companies around the world are investing in robotics to enhance productivity, improve safety, and enrich daily life.

Collaborative Innovation

Cross-industry partnerships are accelerating innovation in robotics. Collaborations between robotics companies, AI developers, and industry leaders are fostering the development of more robust and versatile robots. Open-source development and sharing knowledge can lead to breakthroughs that benefit everyone.

Your Role in the Robotics Revolution

As these technologies develop, individuals can play a role by staying informed and engaging in discussions about the ethical use of robots and their impact on society. Exploring educational opportunities in robotics, programming, or AI can prepare you to be part of this emerging field.

Reflection Questions

How comfortable are you with the idea of humanoid robots becoming part of everyday life, both at work and at home?

What ethical considerations do you think are most important as we integrate robots into society?

In what ways might humanoid robots enhance or challenge human relationships and social interactions?

Chapter 4: The Age of Plenitude

Embracing Abundance in an Automated World

Imagine a future where the basic needs of every person on the planet are met abundantly. Clean water flows freely, food is plentiful, energy is affordable and renewable, and housing is accessible to all. This is not a utopian fantasy but a potential reality as we stand on the brink of an era shaped by advanced artificial intelligence (AI) and robotics. This new epoch is often referred to as the "Age of Plenitude."

From Post-Scarcity to Plenitude

The term "post-scarcity" has been used to describe a future where goods, services, and resources are universally available in unlimited quantities. However, this concept isn't entirely accurate. Certain things will always remain scarce. For example, there will never be more than twenty paintings by Leonardo da Vinci. We might replicate his style using AI and create perfect imitations, but the original works are finite and irreplaceable.

Instead, the "Age of Plenitude" is a more precise term to describe a world where most goods and services are abundant, but some unique items remain scarce. High-end resources and premium goods that require a uniquely human touch or are limited by nature will still be rare. However, the essentials for a comfortable life—clean water, nutritious food, energy, and basic shelter—could become accessible to everyone, largely due to advancements in AI and robotics.

Automation and the Transformation of Labor

AI and robotics are advancing at an unprecedented pace. Developments like GPT-4 and the anticipated GPT-5 are pushing the boundaries of what machines can do. The goal of achieving Artificial GeneralIntelligence (AGI)—AI that can perform any intellectual task a human can, and potentially do it better—is on the horizon. Companies like OpenAI, DeepMind, and others are actively pursuing this goal.

As AI becomes more capable, it's poised to automate up to 100% of human labor in certain sectors. Robots and AI systems can work tirelessly around the clock without fatigue, illness, or the need for breaks. They don't require wages in the traditional sense, which can drastically reduce the cost of goods and services.

Imagine factories where AI-powered robots handle manufacturing, assembly, and quality control with precision and efficiency. Automated farms could produce food abundantly without the need for human labor, using AI to optimize growth conditions and yields. In healthcare, AI-driven systems are already transforming the field.

Breakthroughs like DeepMind's AlphaFold, which solved the complex problem of protein folding, are accelerating drug discovery and bringing us closer to personalized medicine. AI could also diagnose and treat patients with even greater accuracy than human doctors by analyzing vast amounts of medical data, ensuring timely and effective care.

Energy Revolution: Powering the Age of Plenitude

Achieving the Age of Plenitude isn't possible without a significant shift in how we produce and consume energy. Renewable energy sources like solar and wind have become increasingly affordable. Between 2010 and 2020, the cost of renewable energy dropped by 82%. By 2041, it's predicted that much of the developed world and even developing countries will be powered primarily by renewable energy.

There's also the potential breakthrough of nuclear fusion—a process that could generate energy that's four million times more efficient than burning oil or coal. While nuclear fusion has been an elusive goal for decades, continued research brings us closer to this transformative energy source.

With abundant, clean energy, we can power the AI systems and robotics that will drive production and services in the Age of Plenitude. This synergy between renewable energy and advanced technology is key to creating a sustainable and abundant future.

Dematerialization and Accessibility

Peter Diamandis, a prominent futurist, refers to the concept of "dematerialization," where physical products become obsolete as digital and virtual alternatives take their place. Items like radios, cameras, maps, and GPS systems have already been transformed into apps on our smartphones. As AI and technology continue to evolve, expensive products and services will become cheap or even free, increasing accessibility worldwide.

Virtual reality (VR) and AI could provide immersive experiences and entertainment at a fraction of the current cost. Education could be revolutionized with AI tutors providing personalized learning experiences to students globally. Medical consultations and mental health support could become widely accessible through AI-driven platforms.

Meeting Basic Human Needs

One of the most profound impacts of the Age of Plenitude is the potential to meet basic human needs on a global scale:

Clean Water: Today, approximately 2 billion people lack access to clean drinking water. AI and robotics can revolutionize water purification and distribution systems, making clean water available to all.

Food Production: Automated farms and advances in synthetic biology could produce food abundantly and sustainably. AI can engineer bacteria to supply essential nutrients to plants, reducing the need for harmful chemical fertilizers.

Housing: AI-powered construction robots could assemble homes quickly and efficiently, reducing housing shortages and making shelter affordable.

Energy: With advancements in renewable energy and potential breakthroughs like nuclear fusion, clean and affordable energy could become the norm.

Reimagining the Economy

As AI and robotics automate labor, the traditional economic models based on human work and wages will need to be reevaluated. If machines handle the majority of production and services, how will people earn income? How will wealth be distributed?

This transition presents both challenges and opportunities:

Universal Basic Income (UBI): Some propose UBI as a solution, providing everyone with a baseline income regardless of employment. This could help people meet their basic needs while they pursue education, creativity, or entrepreneurial endeavors.

Redefining Work: Work may shift from being a necessity for survival to a means of personal fulfillment. People might choose careers based on passion rather than financial need.

Education and Reskilling: Emphasis on education could grow, with people encouraged to develop skills in areas where human creativity and emotional intelligence are valuable.

Ethical Considerations and Avoiding Pitfalls

While the Age of Plenitude offers immense promise, it's essential to navigate the ethical considerations carefully:

Preventing Inequality: Without proper management, the benefits of automation could concentrate wealth among those who own the machines, exacerbating economic inequality.

Avoiding Human Greed: Developing new economic models requires a focus on fairness and abundance rather than profit maximization. Policies and regulations need to ensure that technological advancements benefit society as a whole.

Ensuring Meaningful Engagement: With basic needs met, people might struggle with purpose and motivation. Societal emphasis on personal growth, community involvement, and the arts could help individuals find meaning beyond traditional employment.

Seizing Opportunities and Preparing for the Future

The coming era calls for proactive engagement from all of us:

Embrace Lifelong Learning: Continuously updating skills and knowledge will be crucial. Fields like arts, philosophy, science, and social work, where human touch is irreplaceable, may flourish.

Cultivate Creativity and Innovation: With automation handling routine tasks, there's greater space for creative endeavors. This could lead to a cultural renaissance in arts, literature, and innovation.

Participate in Dialogue: Engaging in conversations about the future economy, ethical use of AI, and societal values is essential. Public input can help shape policies that reflect the needs and desires of the community.

Foster Resilience and Adaptability: Change can be challenging. Building personal resilience and adaptability will help individuals navigate the transitions ahead.

The Role of Policymakers and Society

Governments and institutions have a critical role to play:

Developing Inclusive Policies: Crafting regulations that ensure equitable distribution of resources and opportunities is vital.

Investing in Education: Supporting educational initiatives that prepare people for a changing world can empower individuals and strengthen societies.**Promoting Ethical AI Development**: Establishing guidelines for AI and robotics to ensure they are developed and used responsibly.

Conclusion: Building a Future of Abundance

The Age of Plenitude holds the potential for unprecedented human advancement. By harnessing AI and robotics responsibly, we can create a world where basic needs are met, opportunities abound, and people are free to pursue meaningful endeavors.

This future isn't guaranteed, and it won't happen automatically. It requires conscious effort, ethical considerations, and collaborative action. Each of us has a role to play—whether it's staying informed, participating in discussions, or taking initiative to seize new opportunities.

As we stand on the cusp of this new era, let's embrace the possibilities with optimism and determination. Together, we can shape a future that not only leverages technological advancements but also uplifts humanity.

Reflection Questions

How can we ensure that the benefits of automation and AI are distributed equitably across society?

What steps can you take to prepare for a future where traditional labor is transformed or reduced?

In a world where basic needs are met, what would give your life meaning and purpose?

How can communities foster a culture that values creativity, learning, and social connections in the Age of Plenitude?

Chapter 5: Human Jobs in an Automated World

Adapting to Change and Embracing New Opportunities

Artificial Intelligence (AI) is rapidly transforming the landscape of work. Every day brings new headlines about AI advancements—some heralding unprecedented opportunities, others warning of potential job losses.

For example, tools like GitHub Copilot are already assisting software developers by writing routine code, allowing them to focus on more creative, complex tasks. In content creation, AI tools like Jasper are helping writers generate ideas and first drafts, streamlining processes that once took hours. These tools are reshaping how people work across industries, highlighting that AI often augments rather than eliminates human roles. With reasoning models like OpenAI's o1 model poised to make true agents available we will continue to see productivity supercharged.

Amid this whirlwind of change, it's natural to wonder: What does AI mean for our jobs, our careers, and our futures?

To navigate these questions, let's delve into recent research and discussions from the AI and the Future of Work conference held at Georgetown University. This gathering of leading AI researchers and experts shed light on how AI is impacting the job market, the nature of work, and what it means for workers across various industries.

Tracking AI's Influence Through Patents

One innovative approach to understanding AI's impact is by examining patent filings. Patents serve as public records of technological advancements, offering a tangible way to trace the development and implementation of AI technologies.Researchers analyzed patents filed by companies investing heavily in AI. They discovered that these companies are experiencing significant boosts in productivity—not just in isolated areas but across their entire operations.

This includes:

Labor Productivity: Increases in the amount of output produced per worker.

Total Factor Productivity: Improvements considering all inputs, including technology, capital, and labor.

Interestingly, the study found no statistically significant negative impact on income inequality within these companies. While this is encouraging, it's important to note that these companies represent the cutting edge of AI adoption. Their experiences may not reflect the broader economy, especially in sectors where AI is not yet as prevalent.

The Rise of "Linchpin" Workers and AI Assistance

Another insightful study focused on software developers, particularly those considered "linchpin workers." These are highly skilled individuals essential to a project's success, often holding teams together with their expertise. These linchpin developers frequently find themselves bogged down with tasks outside their core competencies, such as administrative duties or dealing with inefficient software tools. Researchers explored what would happen if these key workers were provided with AI assistants—specifically, tools like GitHub Copilot, an AI that can assist with coding.

The results were significant:

Enhanced Focus on Core Tasks: With AI handling routine coding tasks, developers could concentrate on complex problem-solving and creative work.

Improved Productivity: The AI assistant helped reduce time spent on debugging and code search, streamlining workflows.

Skill Development for Less Experienced Coders: Less experienced developers benefited from AI assistance, effectively receiving on-the-spot tutoring that accelerated their learning.

This suggests that AI can enhance individual productivity and team efficiency, leading to potential shifts in team dynamics and organizational structures.

Redefining Team Dynamics and Management Roles

As AI takes on more routine and administrative tasks, traditional team structures may evolve:

Flatter Hierarchies: With AI managing certain coordination tasks, teams might operate with fewer managerial layers, leading to more autonomy and flexibility.

Evolving Management Roles: Managers may shift from overseeing day-to-day operations to focusing on strategic leadership, mentorship, and fostering innovation.

Enhanced Collaboration: AI tools can facilitate better communication and coordination among team members, regardless of their physical location.

However, these changes raise important questions about the future of management and leadership. If AI handles many traditional managerial tasks, what does that mean for those roles? While some positions may change significantly or become obsolete, new opportunities may arise in areas where human skills are irreplaceable.

AI as a General-Purpose Technology

A pivotal discussion at the conference centered on whether AI, particularly large language models like GPT-4, represents a "General-Purpose Technology" (GPT) akin to electricity or the internet—technologies that fundamentally transform economies and societies.

Researchers analyzed real job descriptions from the Bureau of Labor Statistics to assess how existing AI models could impact various occupations. Their findings indicated that:

Broad Applicability: AI has the potential to boost productivity across a wide range of jobs without extensive customization.

Immediate Potential: The capabilities of current AI models are sufficient to enhance productivity today, not just in the distant future.

Impact on High-Paying Jobs: Higher-paying positions are more likely to experience significant productivity gains from AI integration.

This underscores the transformative potential of AI across the economy, highlighting both opportunities and challenges.

Addressing Inequality and Ensuring Inclusive Benefits

While AI offers substantial productivity gains, it also raises concerns about widening the gap between those who benefit and those who may be left behind:

Risk of Increased Inequality: If higher-paying jobs gain more from AI, existing income disparities could worsen.

Need for Reskilling and Upskilling: Workers may need access to education and training to adapt to new tools and remain competitive. Ideas proposed like programs that would offer public sector employment or provide free or subsidized education and training to help workers adapt to new technologies.

Importance of Safety Nets: As AI and automation reshape industries and potentially displace jobs, social policies may be necessary to support those adversely affected by technological transitions. One such idea is Universal Basic Income (UBI), a system where the government provides a regular, unconditional payment to every citizen.

The concept of UBI has gained traction in recent years as a potential solution to the economic disruption caused by automation. By providing a financial safety net, UBI aims to ensure that all individuals have the means to meet their basic needs, even if traditional employment becomes less stable. This would not only help individuals transition into new roles but also support personal development, creativity, and entrepreneurship by removing the constant pressure to earn a living through labor.

By implementing a combination of UBI and reskilling efforts, governments can help smooth the transition into a more automated economy, ensuring that the benefits of technological progress are shared by all members of society. Ensuring that AI's benefits are broadly shared requires proactive efforts from businesses, governments, and educational institutions.

Embracing Change and Lifelong Learning

The AI revolution is not a distant possibility; it's unfolding now. Adapting to this new landscape involves:

Staying Curious: Keeping abreast of technological advancements helps individuals anticipate changes and seize new opportunities.

Developing New Skills: Embracing lifelong learning is essential. Skills like critical thinking, creativity, emotional intelligence, and adaptability are increasingly valuable.

Collaborating with AI: Viewing AI as a tool to enhance human capabilities rather than a threat can lead to more productive and fulfilling work experiences.

By working with AI, we can amplify our strengths and focus on tasks that require uniquely human qualities.

Reimagining the Future of Work

The integration of AI into the workplace presents an opportunity to rethink traditional notions of work. Rather than viewing AI as a threat, we can see it as a tool that empowers employees and unlocks new opportunities for creativity and innovation.

Redefining Roles:

As AI takes over routine and repetitive tasks, job descriptions and responsibilities will evolve, with a focus on skills that machines cannot easily replicate—such as emotional intelligence, complex problem-solving, and creative thinking. This shift will allow workers to focus on more meaningful and impactful contributions, transforming work into a space for innovation and personal growth.

Flexible Work Structures:

Organizations may adopt more fluid team arrangements, moving away from rigid hierarchies to more agile and collaborative models. AI tools can enhance communication, streamline workflows, and enable faster decision-making, allowing teams to respond to challenges and opportunities in real-time. With AI handling administrative tasks, employees will have more freedom to focus on strategic and creative efforts, promoting a culture of flexibility and adaptability.

Empowering Employees:

By democratizing access to AI tools, workers at all levels will be able to leverage advanced technologies to perform their jobs more effectively. From AI-driven data analysis to automated customer support systems, employees will have powerful tools at their disposal to enhance productivity, improve decision-making, and reduce time spent on tedious tasks. This empowerment can lead to higher job satisfaction, as workers will feel more in control of their roles and better equipped to succeed in a tech-enhanced workplace.

This shift invites us to envision a future where technology doesn't replace human workers but instead enhances human potential. As AI becomes an integral part of the workforce, it can free us from mundane tasks, allowing for more innovation, creativity, and meaningful human interactions. The future of work, shaped by AI, has the potential to uplift employees by making work more engaging and impactful.

Reflection Questions

How might AI tools enhance or change the tasks you perform in your own job or field of interest?

What steps can you take to develop skills that complement AI technologies rather than compete with them?

How can society support workers in transitioning to new roles as AI transforms traditional job functions?

Chapter 6: Navigating AI Ethics and Creativity

Shaping the Future Through Dialogue and Innovation

Artificial Intelligence is no longer a distant concept confined to science fiction; it's a pervasive force that's rapidly transforming our world. From voice assistants on our phones to recommendation algorithms on our favorite streaming services, AI is integrated into our daily lives in ways we might not even realize. As we navigate this new landscape, it's crucial to cut through the hype and understand what AI means for us right now.

The Ethical Dimensions of AI

The ethical considerations surrounding AI are immediate and pressing. AI systems are making decisions that affect our lives, often without our explicit awareness. These decisions range from which news articles appear in our social media feeds to more critical outcomes like loan approvals or medical diagnoses.

One of the challenges in regulating AI is its operation on what experts call "machine time." Unlike humans, AI can process and analyze vast amounts of data in fractions of a second. For example, an AI algorithm trading stocks can execute thousands of transactions in the time it takes for a person to blink. This speed and scale make traditional regulatory approaches difficult to apply.

Moreover, AI doesn't think like humans. It lacks consciousness and emotions, which means it doesn't have an inherent understanding of human values or ethics. This disparity raises questions about how we ensure AI systems act in ways that align with societal norms and moral principles.

The Role of AI Enthusiasts and the Community

While governments and large tech companies play significant roles in shaping AI's trajectory, there's a growing community of AI enthusiasts, researchers, and developers who are pushing the boundaries of what these technologies can do. These individuals often experiment with AI in innovative ways, discovering new applications and uncovering potential issues that might not be evident in controlled corporate environments.

This grassroots movement is reminiscent of the early days of the internet when individuals and small groups explored the possibilities of a new digital frontier.

Today, AI enthusiasts contribute to the field by:

Experimenting Creatively: They use AI models in unanticipated ways, such as employing language processing algorithms to compose complex music or generate visual art.

Identifying Ethical Concerns: By testing the limits of AI systems, they help reveal biases, limitations, and vulnerabilities that need to be addressed.

Sharing Knowledge: Through open-source projects, forums, and collaborations, they disseminate findings that accelerate the collective understanding of AI.

AI as a Tool for Creativity

Contrary to the notion of AI as a cold, calculating entity, it is increasingly becoming a catalyst for human creativity. AI can serve as a "creative mirror," reflecting and amplifying our cultural expressions. Artists, musicians, writers, and designers are leveraging AI to explore new frontiers in their work. But what's even more remarkable is how AI opens the door for those who may not have considered themselves naturally gifted in the arts to now express themselves like never before.

AI tools are making creativity more accessible, offering people without formal training or artistic backgrounds the ability to compose music, generate stunning visual art, write stories, and even design complex structures with ease. By collaborating with AI, individuals are discovering hidden creative potential, allowing them to produce works they may have never imagined possible.

Personally, I've found that working with AI has expanded my own creativity and productivity. AI acts as a powerful creative partner, offering suggestions, refining ideas, and helping bring to life visions that were once difficult to realize. This democratization of creativity means that whether you're a seasoned artist or someone who simply wants to express a creative idea, AI provides a platform for everyone to explore, create, and share their unique perspectives with the world.

For instance:

Music Composition:

Musicians are increasingly using AI to generate melodies, harmonies, and even entire compositions, inspiring fresh musical directions and unexpected collaborations. It's not about replacing artists; it's about opening the door for more people to join the creative process. AI allows individuals who may not have formal musical training to express themselves musically, creating new opportunities for innovation and experimentation.

Visual Arts:

Artists are leveraging AI to create unique artworks, experiment with different styles, and even co-create pieces as partners with the technology. AI-generated visual art is emerging as a vibrant new medium, offering creators —from professionals to amateurs—an additional outlet for expression. This technology empowers more people to explore the visual arts, regardless of their technical skills, and push the boundaries of traditional artistic forms.

Literature and Writing:

Writers are turning to AI not just to overcome writer's block, but also to generate new ideas, explore alternative narratives, and enhance their storytelling. Beyond that, AI assists in proofreading, suggesting edits, and automating formatting, streamlining the entire creative process. Rather than replacing writers, AI enhances their ability to craft compelling stories while making the tools of professional writing more accessible to everyone.

These tools do not replace human creativity but enhance it, providing new mediums and methods to express ideas. They can analyze vast amounts of existing work, identify patterns, and suggest novel combinations that might not have been apparent otherwise.

The Importance of Open Dialogue

As AI becomes more integrated into society, it's essential to foster open and inclusive conversations about its implications. These discussions should extend beyond technical experts and policymakers to include people from all walks of life.

Here are some ways to promote meaningful dialogue:

Use Relatable Examples: Instead of diving into complex technical jargon, start conversations with everyday instances of AI, such as navigation apps, streaming service recommendations, or virtual assistants.

Acknowledge Both Sides: Recognize the potential benefits of AI, like advancements in healthcare and education, while also addressing valid concerns such as job displacement and privacy issues.

Encourage Questions: Create an environment where people feel comfortable asking questions and expressing their thoughts without fear of judgment.

Share Personal Experiences: Discuss how AI impacts your own life, both positively and negatively, to make the topic more tangible.
Effective communication about AI helps demystify the technology, reduces fear of the unknown, and empowers individuals to participate in shaping its future.

Balancing Optimism with Realism

It's important to maintain a balanced perspective on AI:

Optimism: Embrace the exciting possibilities that AI offers for innovation, problem-solving, and improving quality of life.

Realism: Stay aware of the challenges and ethical dilemmas that accompany technological advancements.
By acknowledging both the opportunities and the risks, we can work towards solutions that maximize benefits while mitigating downsides.

Shaping the Future Together

AI's trajectory isn't set in stone; it's being written every day by developers, users, policymakers, and communities worldwide. Each of us has a role to play in this unfolding story.

Active Participation: Engage with AI technologies thoughtfully, providing feedback and sharing experiences to inform better designs and policies.

Ethical Consideration: Advocate for responsible AI development that prioritizes fairness, transparency, and respect for human rights

Lifelong Learning: Stay informed about AI trends and developments to make knowledgeable decisions and contributions.

By collaborating and communicating effectively, we can guide AI towards outcomes that reflect our shared values and aspirations. As we navigate the rapidly changing world shaped by AI, let us remember that technology reflects the intentions and values of those who create and use it. By approaching AI with curiosity, responsibility, and a commitment to collective well-being, we can harness its potential to enrich our lives and build a future that aligns with our highest ideals.

Reflection Questions

How has AI already impacted your daily life in ways you might not have previously recognized?

What are your primary concerns about the increasing integration of AI into society, and how might these be addressed?

In what ways can AI serve as a tool to enhance your own creativity or work?

How can you contribute to open and balanced conversations about AI with friends, family, or colleagues?

Chapter 7: The Intelligence Age

Embracing Superintelligence and Shaping Our Future

Imagine a world where artificial intelligence surpasses human intelligence in nearly every domain. This isn't a scene from a science fiction novel but a potential reality we are approaching—a new era referred to as the "Intelligence Age." Just as the Agricultural and Industrial Revolutions fundamentally transformed society, the Intelligence Age promises to redefine our lives in profound ways.

From Deep Learning to Superintelligence

At the heart of this transformation is a breakthrough in AI known as deep learning. Deep learning involves teaching computers to learn and make decisions similarly to how humans do, but with the capacity to process and analyze vast amounts of data at speeds we cannot match. This enables AI systems to find patterns and solutions that might elude human researchers.

Consider the humble grain of sand. Through technological advancements, we've transformed sand into silicon chips—the building blocks of modern computers. These chips power AI systems that are rapidly advancing toward superintelligence—AI that can outperform humans across a wide range of tasks.

Experts are both amazed and cautious about the potential of superintelligence. AI-powered initiatives like Google's AI for Earth are already making strides in addressing climate change by optimizing land use and improving resource management. Similarly, AI-driven weather prediction models are providing more accurate forecasts, helping communities prepare for and mitigate the effects of extreme weather events. While it holds the promise of solving complex global challenges, it also raises questions about control, ethics, and the role of humanity in a world where machines possess superior intelligence.

An Optimistic Vision for the Future

Despite the uncertainties, there's a growing sense of optimism about what the Intelligence Age could bring. Rather than fearing a dystopian future dominated by machines, many envision a world where AI fosters shared prosperity and enhances human well-being.

Equitable Access to Resources

AI has the potential to democratize access to essential resources:

Healthcare: AI-driven diagnostics and personalized medicine could make high-quality healthcare accessible to people worldwide, regardless of their location or economic status.

Education: Imagine every student having a personal AI tutor available 24/7, adapting to their learning style, identifying strengths and weaknesses, and providing customized support. This could revolutionize education by ensuring that everyone has the opportunity to reach their full potential.

Sustainable Energy and Environment: AI can optimize energy use, develop renewable energy solutions, and address environmental challenges, contributing to a healthier planet.

To realize this optimistic future, several key elements must be in place. First, significant advancements in computing power are necessary to support the complex AI systems that will drive future innovations. Equally important is the development of sustainable energy sources to power these AI systems efficiently and at scale, particularly as AI's computational demands grow. Lastly, fostering the right human will—a collective commitment to ethical AI development and global collaboration—will ensure that these technologies are used responsibly and for the benefit of all humanity.

The Pillars of the Intelligence Age

Compute Power: Advanced AI requires significant computational resources. Investing in the infrastructure to support AI development is crucial. This includes data centers, high-performance processors, and networks capable of handling massive amounts of information.

Energy: Running powerful AI systems demands substantial energy. Advancements in renewable energy sources and energy-efficient technologies are essential to sustainably power the Intelligence Age.

Human Will: Perhaps most importantly, the direction AI takes depends on human choices. Collective willpower and ethical considerations will shape how AI is developed and applied. This involves international cooperation, responsible governance, and a commitment to using AI for the common good.

Navigating Challenges and Avoiding Conflicts

As with any transformative technology, there are potential pitfalls:

Geopolitical Tensions:

Competition over AI supremacy could lead to significant conflicts between nations, as countries vie for technological dominance and strategic advantages. This competition could escalate tensions, especially in areas like military applications, economic influence, and cybersecurity. The risk is that an AI arms race, similar to past nuclear or space races, could emerge, with potentially destabilizing consequences. To avoid this, it is critical to foster international collaboration rather than rivalry. Establishing global AI governance frameworks—focused on transparency, ethical use, and shared technological advancements—can help ensure that AI serves the broader interests of humanity, rather than just a few powerful states. Collaborative efforts in AI research, regulation, and ethical standards will be key to diffusing these tensions and ensuring that AI benefits all, not just those who reach technological supremacy first.

Corporate Control:

If a small number of corporations monopolize AI technology, the economic and social disparities could widen drastically. This concentration of power could lead to situations where only the wealthiest companies and nations benefit from AI's vast potential, leaving smaller players, underdeveloped regions, and average citizens at a significant disadvantage. This monopolization could limit access to AI innovations and reinforce economic inequalities, as fewer entities control the means of production and the wealth generated from AI-driven industries.

Policies promoting openness, fair competition, and shared access to AI technologies are essential to prevent this scenario. Encouraging open-source AI development and ensuring that smaller businesses, researchers, and governments can access AI tools without prohibitive costs can help democratize AI's benefits.

Public-private partnerships and strong antitrust regulations could also ensure that AI development remains accessible to a broader range of stakeholders.

Ethical Concerns:

The rapid growth of AI raises profound ethical concerns that need to be addressed proactively to avoid unintended consequences. Issues like data privacy, bias in decision-making algorithms, accountability for AI actions, and the transparency of AI systems are at the forefront of these discussions. AI systems can inadvertently reinforce societal biases if trained on biased data, leading to unjust outcomes in areas like hiring, law enforcement, or financial services.

Moreover, as AI systems become more integrated into critical infrastructure and decision-making processes, accountability becomes a pressing issue—who is responsible if an AI system causes harm? Establishing ethical frameworks and regulations is essential to guide AI development responsibly. Governments, businesses, and international organizations must work together to create standards that promote fairness, accountability, and transparency, ensuring that AI systems are not only effective but also just and equitable. Furthermore, public involvement in these discussions is crucial to ensure that AI's development aligns with societal values and rights.

The Future of Work in the Intelligence Age

One of the most common concerns about AI is its impact on employment. Will machines render human workers obsolete? History provides valuable insights.

The Elevator Operator Analogy:

In the early 20th century, elevator operators were an essential part of daily life in office buildings and hotels, manually controlling the machinery to ensure safe travel between floors. However, with the invention of automatic elevators, these jobs gradually disappeared. Instead of leading to widespread unemployment, this shift freed workers to pursue more complex, creative, and higher-skilled roles, while the automation of elevators became a symbol of technological progress.

As with elevator operators, the rise of AI and automation may eliminate certain jobs, but it also opens the door for new opportunities and industries that are yet to be imagined.

Similarly, while AI may automate certain tasks or even entire professions, it will also create new opportunities:

Evolving Roles:

As AI takes over routine and repetitive tasks, the roles humans fill in the workplace are expected to evolve, with a stronger focus on tasks that require creativity, emotional intelligence, and complex problem-solving—areas where humans naturally excel. While machines can process vast amounts of data and execute predictable tasks, they lack the intuition, empathy, and adaptability needed for nuanced roles in fields like leadership, counseling, creative arts, and strategy.

This shift presents an opportunity for workers to move away from monotonous jobs and into more meaningful, people-centric roles where human insight is invaluable. As a result, workplaces will increasingly value skills that blend technical expertise with soft skills like collaboration, ethical judgment, and creativity, ensuring that humans remain at the heart of decision-making in a world increasingly shaped by technology.

New Industries:

Just as the rise of the internet brought about entirely new sectors—like social media management, app development, and digital marketing—AI is poised to give rise to industries we haven't even conceived yet. As AI continues to unlock new technological possibilities, it will create demand for roles that require a deep understanding of how AI can be applied in areas ranging from healthcare and education to entertainment and environmental sustainability.

AI ethics, data governance, machine learning education, and human-AI collaboration design are just a few examples of emerging fields that could blossom into thriving industries. Additionally, as AI reshapes existing sectors, workers will need to adapt by learning new skills that complement these technologies, creating new career pathways for individuals ready to take on the opportunities of this next wave of innovation.

Enhancing Human Capabilities:

Far from replacing human workers, AI has the potential to augment human abilities, allowing us to achieve more than ever before. By handling data analysis, automation, and decision-making tasks, AI frees up humans to focus on higher-level thinking, creativity, and complex problem-solving. For example, AI can help medical professionals analyze patient data more quickly and accurately, allowing doctors to focus on patient care and innovative treatments. Similarly, AI-driven design tools enable architects and engineers to push the boundaries of creativity, exploring designs that would have been too complex or time-consuming to develop manually. This collaboration between humans and AI enables us to amplify our natural strengths—creativity, empathy, and strategic thinking—while reducing the burden of repetitive or time-consuming tasks, making us more productive, innovative, and fulfilled in our work.

Embracing Collaboration Between Humans and AI

Rather than viewing AI as a competitor, we can see it as a collaborator:

Amplifying Creativity: AI can assist artists, writers, and musicians in exploring new creative avenues.

Enhancing Decision-Making: In fields like healthcare and finance, AI can provide data-driven insights to support human judgment.

Improving Quality of Life: By automating mundane tasks, AI frees up time for people to pursue passions, spend time with loved ones, and engage in lifelong learning. Being more creative, making better decisions, living a quality life are goals we can all embrace.

Imagining the Possibilities

As we stand on the threshold of the Intelligence Age, it's inspiring to consider the vast array of problems that superintelligent AI could help us solve. The potential applications are profound, touching every aspect of human life and the planet we inhabit.

Eradicating Diseases

One of the most promising possibilities is the eradication of diseases. Superintelligent AI could revolutionize medical research by accelerating the discovery of cures and treatments at an unprecedented pace. For example, AI could analyze vast datasets of genetic information to identify the underlying causes of diseases like cancer or Alzheimer's. By modeling complex biological processes, AI could predict how diseases progress and how they might be halted or reversed.

During global health crises, such as pandemics, AI could expedite vaccine development by simulating how viruses mutate and how the human immune system responds. This could lead to the creation of effective vaccines and treatments in a fraction of the time it currently takes.

Moreover, AI-driven diagnostics could enable early detection of illnesses through analysis of medical images or biomarkers, improving patient outcomes through timely intervention.

Imagine a world where diseases like malaria, tuberculosis, and HIV/AIDS are no longer threats because AI has helped develop effective treatments and prevention strategies. By tailoring medical care to individual genetic profiles, AI could usher in an era of personalized medicine, improving the efficacy of treatments and reducing side effects.

Ending Hunger

Another critical area where AI could make a transformative impact is in ending global hunger. By optimizing food production and distribution, AI has the potential to ensure that everyone has access to sufficient, nutritious food.

For instance, AI-powered systems could assist farmers by analyzing soil conditions, weather patterns, and crop health to recommend the optimal timing for planting, irrigation, and harvesting. This precision agriculture approach could significantly increase crop yields and reduce resource waste.

In addition, AI could enhance supply chain efficiency by predicting demand, reducing spoilage, and improving logistics. For example, machine learning algorithms could forecast food consumption trends, allowing producers and distributors to adjust accordingly. In regions prone to food insecurity, AI could help identify the most vulnerable populations and coordinate relief efforts more effectively, ensuring that aid reaches those who need it most.

Consider a scenario where small-scale farmers in developing countries use affordable AI tools to maximize their harvests, contributing to local food security and economic growth. AI could also aid in developing resilient crop varieties that withstand climate change impacts, safeguarding food supplies for future generations.

Combating Climate Change

Combating climate change is perhaps one of the most pressing challenges of our time, and AI could play a pivotal role in developing innovative solutions to reduce emissions and restore ecosystems. Superintelligent AI could help design advanced renewable energy technologies, such as more efficient solar panels or energy storage systems, making clean energy more accessible and affordable.

AI could also optimize energy consumption across industries by analyzing usage patterns and recommending efficiency improvements. For example, smart grids powered by AI could balance energy supply and demand in real-time, reducing waste and lowering carbon footprints.

In transportation, AI could enhance the efficiency of electric vehicles and public transit systems, reducing reliance on fossil fuels.
In environmental conservation, AI could process satellite imagery and sensor data to monitor deforestation, glacier melting, and ocean health. By identifying critical areas in need of protection or restoration, AI could guide conservation efforts with greater precision. Additionally, AI models could simulate the effects of various climate interventions, helping policymakers choose the most effective strategies to mitigate environmental damage.
Imagine cities designed with the help of AI to be more sustainable and livable, with optimized traffic flows, green spaces, and efficient resource management.

AI could also facilitate global cooperation by providing transparent data on environmental impacts, fostering collaborative efforts to address climate change.

Our Role in Shaping the Intelligence Age

The future isn't something that simply happens to us; it's something we actively create. Each of us has a role to play in guiding the development of AI:

Engagement: Stay informed about AI advancements and participate in discussions about their implications. As AI continues to reshape industries, societies, and economies, it's critical for individuals
to remain engaged with the latest developments.

This can involve attending conferences, reading relevant publications, or simply staying updated on how AI is being applied in fields ranging from healthcare to transportation. By actively participating in discussions—whether in your local community or online—you can help shape public understanding and policy decisions, ensuring that AI development reflects the values and needs of society

Advocacy: Support policies and initiatives that promote ethical AI, equitable access, and sustainable practices. AI has the power to create vast societal benefits, but it also poses risks if left unchecked. Advocacy for responsible AI means championing regulations that ensure transparency, fairness, and accountability in AI systems. This could include pushing for AI systems that avoid bias, promote data privacy, and are accessible to all sectors of society, not just the wealthy or technologically advanced.
Engaging with policymakers, signing petitions, or supporting organizations that promote ethical AI can help ensure these technologies benefit everyone and foster a more just and inclusive future.

Education: Embrace lifelong learning to adapt to changing job landscapes and acquire new skills. AI is rapidly transforming the nature of work, making it essential for individuals to continue learning throughout their lives.

Whether it's through formal education, online courses, or self-guided study, staying up-to-date on emerging technologies and learning new skills can help individuals remain competitive in an evolving workforce. Skills in AI, data analysis, programming, and even soft skills like creativity and emotional intelligence will be highly valuable in a future where machines increasingly handle routine tasks. By prioritizing education, you ensure that you're equipped to thrive in an AI-driven world.

Collaboration: Work together across disciplines, industries, and cultures to address the challenges and opportunities of AI. No single person or field can manage the complexities of AI development and its impact on society. Scientists, engineers, policymakers, ethicists, business leaders, and the general public all have a role to play in shaping AI's future.

Collaborative efforts—whether through partnerships between tech companies and governments, or cross-disciplinary academic research—will be key to addressing AI's challenges. By fostering a spirit of cooperation and leveraging the expertise of diverse groups, we can ensure that AI is developed in ways that are innovative, ethical, and beneficial to all

Imagining Your Impact

As we envision the possibilities, consider how you might contribute to this transformative era. Perhaps you're inspired to pursue a career in AI research, or maybe you see opportunities to apply AI solutions in your community. The Intelligence Age invites each of us to imagine the problems we can solve and the improvements we can make in the world.

On our journey into this new era, let us embrace the potential of superintelligent AI with optimism tempered by wisdom. By working together, we can harness this transformative technology to build a future that reflects our highest aspirations—a world where innovation and humanity thrive in harmony.

Reflection Questions

What aspects of the Intelligence Age excite you the most, and why?

How can we ensure that the benefits of superintelligent AI are shared globally and do not exacerbate existing inequalities?

In what ways can you contribute to shaping an ethical and inclusive future in the Intelligence Age?

If AI could solve any problem in the world, which one would you prioritize, and what impact would that have on society?

Chapter 8: The Ethics and Governance of AI

Insights from Industry Leaders on Navigating the AI Revolution
The rapid advancement of Artificial Intelligence (AI) technology has brought about profound changes in how we live, work, and interact with the world. As AI systems become more capable, questions about their ethical use, regulation, and impact on society have moved to the forefront of public discourse.

To delve deeper into these critical issues, we'll explore insights from industry leaders, including Mustafa Suleyman (CEO of Microsoft AI), Sam Altman (CEO of OpenAI), and Yann LeCun (Chief AI Scientist at Meta), all of whom have shaped the ethical conversation around AI development.

Understanding the Current State of AI

Mustafa Suleyman emphasizes that we are at the beginning of an exponential growth curve in AI capabilities. Technologies that once seemed distant are now becoming reality. This rapid development, evident in the widespread use of models like GPT-4, has reshaped industries and daily life. Over the next decade, Suleyman suggests AI will be deeply embedded into nearly every facet of society.

Sam Altman, CEO of OpenAI, shares a similar vision but frames it within the context of responsibility. Altman highlights that while AI is capable of great innovation, it's essential to address the safety concerns early. He believes AI can augment human intelligence but warns of the risks if not developed with strong governance. Altman has repeatedly advocated for global regulation, cautioning that AI will likely impact many areas, from healthcare to military applications, requiring collaborative efforts across industries and governments.

AI Safety and Ethical Considerations

One of the most pressing concerns is ensuring that AI technologies are developed and deployed safely. While Suleyman advocates for proactive measures to prevent misuse, Yann LeCun of Meta stresses the importance of designing systems that are transparent and explainable. He believes that the complexity of AI means that we must actively work to avoid black-box systems —models whose decision-making processes are not easily interpretable. For LeCun, making AI more interpretable and accountable is crucial in building public trust and ensuring that these systems are aligned with human values.

Suleyman, Altman, and LeCun all agree that AI has the potential for unintended consequences, and that a collective effort is required to establish ethical guidelines and safety protocols to prevent AI from being used in harmful ways, particularly in fields such as security and defense.

The Role of Regulation

Regulation is a key component in ensuring the responsible development of AI. Most leaders in the AI space agree that regulation is not a hindrance but an essential framework that can guide AI development in a way that maximizes benefits while minimizing risks. Sam Altman has been an outspoken proponent of global AI regulation, calling for international bodies to establish standards and oversight to prevent misuse, particularly in areas like autonomous weapons. He suggests that without proper global cooperation, AI could exacerbate geopolitical tensions.

Suleyman uses the automobile industry as an example of how regulation can improve safety and societal benefits, while Yann LeCun adds that over-regulation could stifle innovation. He advocates for a balanced approach where open-source models like Meta's LLaMA promote transparency, but acknowledges that proprietary models still play a crucial role in advancing cutting-edge research.

The European Union's AI Act and the U.S. AI Advancement and Reliability Act of 2024 are early frameworks that attempt to bridge innovation and safety, establishing new testing methods and safety standards for AI systems. Altman suggests that such regulations, if designed thoughtfully, will help steer AI towards ethical uses without sacrificing technological progress.

Balancing Open Source and Proprietary AI

The debate between open-source and proprietary AI models is one of the most contested issues in the field. Yann LeCun advocates strongly for open-source AI, believing that wider access will lead to more innovation and transparency. He suggests that democratizing AI development through open platforms is crucial for preventing monopolies and giving smaller companies and researchers the tools to experiment with AI technologies.

However, Sam Altman and Mustafa Suleyman recognize the value of proprietary models in creating secure, scalable AI applications for industries like healthcare, finance, and defense, where risk management is critical. Altman proposes a hybrid approach, where open-source models drive experimentation and education, while proprietary systems are used in areas that require high levels of security and investment.

AI's Impact on Employment and Education

As AI systems become more capable, their impact on jobs and education is a major concern. While Mustafa Suleyman emphasizes the importance of adaptability and lifelong learning, Sam Altman takes a broader view, predicting that Universal Basic Income (UBI) might become necessary as automation continues to displace jobs. He suggests that AI could free humans from many routine tasks, allowing us to focus on more creative and fulfilling roles, but that this will require a complete overhaul of current economic and social structures.

On education, Yann LeCun emphasizes that AI will augment the way we learn, with personalized AI tutors capable of providing individualized learning paths for students. This will allow education to be more adaptive, fostering critical thinking and problem-solving skills rather than rote memorization. LeCun, like Suleyman, stresses that future workers must develop soft skills such as creativity and emotional intelligence to thrive in an AI-enhanced economy.

Global Cooperation and Competition

Sam Altman echoes Suleyman's call for international cooperation to avoid an AI arms race. Both leaders warn that viewing AI as a zero-sum game will lead to increased tensions between countries, particularly the U.S. and China. Yann LeCun adds that collaboration between nations is essential not only for geopolitical stability, but for addressing global challenges like climate change and healthcare. He suggests that AI could be a force for good, but only if international alliances are built on mutual respect and shared ethical standards.

Misinformation and Disinformation

The rise of AI-generated content has raised significant concerns about misinformation and disinformation. While Mustafa Suleyman remains optimistic that humanity will adapt to this new landscape, Sam Altman stresses the need for robust systems that can detect and combat disinformation more efficiently than the AI systems creating it. Yann LeCun suggests that developing AI literacy among the public will be critical, as people need to be equipped with the tools to critically assess the validity of the content they encounter.

The Future of AI and Humanity's Role

Looking ahead, industry leaders agree that AI will become deeply integrated into daily life. Mustafa Suleyman and Sam Altman both emphasize that humans must remain at the center of decision-making, ensuring that AI serves humanity rather than undermining it. Yann LeCun goes further, suggesting that AI systems with emotional intelligence—capable of interacting in more natural and supportive ways—could enhance education, mental health, and customer service, creating better user experiences.

However, as AI becomes more intelligent and ubiquitous, preserving human oversight will be critical to preventing unintended consequences.

Conclusion: Shaping AI's Trajectory Together

Insights from Mustafa Suleyman, Sam Altman, Yann LeCun, and other industry leaders underscore the complex interplay between technological innovation, ethical considerations, and societal impact. As AI continues to evolve, it's imperative that we collectively navigate its development responsibly. By embracing regulation, fostering global cooperation, and ensuring that diverse voices contribute to the conversation, we can shape a future where AI enhances human well-being and aligns with our values.

Reflection Questions

What are your thoughts on balancing innovation and regulation in AI development?

How can you contribute to shaping the responsible use of AI in your community or workplace?

How can global cooperation be fostered to ensure that AI benefits humanity rather than deepening divides?

Chapter 9: Navigating the AI Revolution

Embracing Change and Ethical Leadership in an Age of Transformation

The world as we know it is undergoing a profound transformation. The advent of advanced artificial intelligence (AI) has brought us to a pivotal moment in history—a singularity where the rules of the game change so drastically that the future becomes difficult to predict. Understanding this trajectory is crucial for individuals and organizations alike to navigate the challenges and opportunities that lie ahead.

The Boiling Frog Analogy: Recognizing the Signs
There's a classic proverb about a frog placed in cold water that is slowly heated. The frog doesn't notice the gradual temperature increase until it's too late. This metaphor illustrates how humans often fail to perceive slow but significant changes in their environment. In the context of AI, many are unaware of just how rapidly technology is advancing and how fundamentally it will alter our lives.

Reflecting on recent history, the global response to the COVID-19 pandemic exemplifies this tendency. Despite numerous warnings and precedents, society was largely unprepared for the crisis. Similarly, the rise of AI is a transformative force that demands our immediate attention and proactive engagement.

From Coding Basics to Deep Learning

The journey of AI began decades ago, with early programmers teaching computers to perform tasks by explicitly coding instructions—a process where human intelligence solved problems and machines executed solutions. However, the turn of the century marked a paradigm shift with the advent of deep learning. Computers started learning in a manner akin to humans: by recognizing patterns through exposure to vast amounts of data.

An illustrative example is the "cat paper" published by researchers at Google in 2009. By analyzing countless frames from YouTube videos, an AI system learned to identify cats without being explicitly programmed to do so. This breakthrough demonstrated that machines could develop their own understanding, processing information in ways that humans might not fully comprehend.

The Netscape Moment of AI

The release of user-friendly AI applications like ChatGPT represents a "Netscape moment"—akin to when the internet became accessible to the general public through web browsers. While AI has been developing for years, it's now entering mainstream consciousness as people interact with these powerful tools directly.

ChatGPT and similar models exhibit remarkable capabilities, performing tasks at intelligence levels comparable to or surpassing human experts in certain areas. They can compose essays, generate code, create art, and engage in complex conversations. This rapid advancement challenges previous assumptions about the limitations of AI and signals a need to reassess our relationship with technology.

The Promise of Abundance and the Risk of Misuse

AI holds the potential to usher in an era of abundance. With enhanced intelligence at our fingertips, we could solve some of humanity's most pressing problems, such as climate change, disease, and resource scarcity. Imagine a world where energy is virtually free, and technology enables unprecedented levels of productivity and innovation.

However, this potential comes with significant challenges. The main concern isn't the technology itself but how humans choose to use it. The values and intentions driving AI development will shape its impact on society. Ethical considerations are paramount to ensure that AI benefits all rather than exacerbating inequalities or causing harm.

Five Key Areas of Impact:

1. Concentration of Power and Wealth

AI can lead to a massive concentration of power and wealth in the hands of those who control the technology. Historically, advancements like agriculture, industrialization, and the information age have amplified the capabilities of those with access to new tools. In the AI era, this effect could be even more pronounced, creating trillionaires and shifting geopolitical dynamics. Organizations and nations that leverage AI effectively may gain significant advantages, leading to increased surveillance, regulation, and control.

2. Job Displacement and Economic Shifts

Automation through AI will transform the job market. Roles that can be performed more efficiently by machines will be at risk, leading to unemployment in certain sectors. However, new opportunities will arise for those who can adapt and work alongside AI. Businesses that embrace AI will outperform those that don't, emphasizing the importance of staying current with technological advancements.

3. Changes in Human Connection

AI's ability to mimic human interaction raises questions about the nature of relationships and communication. Virtual assistants and AI companions could replace human interactions for some, exacerbating feelings of loneliness. On the flip side, genuine human connection may become more valued, providing a competitive edge for businesses and individuals who prioritize authentic engagement.

4. Erosion of Truth and Authenticity

The proliferation of AI-generated content makes it challenging to discern reality from fabrication. Deepfakes, synthetic media, and algorithmically curated information can blur the lines between truth and deception. This environment necessitates a heightened focus on critical thinking, transparency, and authenticity to maintain trust and integrity.

5. Ethical Use and Governance of AI

The trajectory of AI development hinges on ethical considerations. Decisions made today will influence how AI evolves and impacts society. Emphasizing values like honesty, fairness, and respect in AI applications is crucial to prevent misuse and unintended consequences.

Preparing for the Future: Three Essential Skills

To navigate the rapidly changing landscape, individuals and organizations should cultivate three key competencies:

1. Mastering AI Tools

Embrace AI technologies by actively learning and experimenting with them. Familiarize yourself with tools like ChatGPT, and explore how they can enhance your personal and professional capabilities. Continuous learning is vital to stay ahead in an AI-driven world.

2. Seeking Truth and Critical Thinking

Develop the ability to discern accurate information amidst a flood of data and potential misinformation. Question assumptions, verify sources, and engage in deep analysis to uncover the underlying realities. This skill is essential to make informed decisions and maintain authenticity.

3. Fostering Human Connection

Prioritize genuine interactions and relationships. In an era where AI can replicate human-like communication, the value of true human connection becomes even more significant. Businesses and individuals who emphasize empathy, understanding, and personal engagement will stand out.

Embracing Ethical Leadership

The ethical use of AI is not just a technological challenge but a moral one. Leaders in all sectors have a responsibility to guide AI development and application in ways that align with humane values. This includes:

Promoting Transparency: Be open about how AI is used and the data it relies on. Transparency builds trust and allows for accountability.

Ensuring Fairness: Strive to eliminate biases in AI systems that could lead to discrimination or inequality.

Prioritizing Well-being: Use AI to enhance quality of life, focusing on solutions that benefit society as a whole rather than solely pursuing profit or power.

The Path Forward

The AI revolution presents both unprecedented opportunities and challenges. By acknowledging the profound changes underway and actively engaging with them, we can shape a future that leverages AI's potential for the greater good. This requires a collective effort to:

Educate Ourselves and Others: Stay informed about AI developments and share knowledge within your community.

Advocate for Ethical Practices: Support policies and initiatives that promote responsible AI use.

Collaborate Across Disciplines: Work together with experts in technology, ethics, law, and other fields to address complex issues.

Cultivate Resilience and Adaptability: Be prepared to adapt to new realities and embrace lifelong learning.

Conclusion: Choosing the Future We Want

The trajectory of AI is not predetermined. While the technology will continue to advance, the impact it has on society depends on our choices. By prioritizing ethical considerations, fostering genuine human connections, and embracing a mindset of abundance rather than scarcity, we can guide AI toward outcomes that benefit everyone.

The question we must ask ourselves is: Will we use AI to create a world of prosperity and harmony, or will we allow short-sighted pursuits to lead us astray? The responsibility lies with each of us to act thoughtfully and intentionally as we navigate this transformative era. As we move forward, let's commit to being proactive stewards of AI technology, ensuring that it serves as a catalyst for positive change. By embracing ethical leadership and fostering a collaborative spirit, we can navigate the complexities of the AI revolution and build a future that reflects our highest values and aspirations.

Reflection Questions

- **How can you integrate AI tools into your work or personal life to enhance your capabilities while maintaining ethical standards?**

- **What steps can you take to improve your ability to discern truth in an age of information overload and potential misinformation?**

- **In what ways can you strengthen genuine human connections in your community or organization amidst increasing digital interactions?**

- **How can leaders promote a culture of ethical AI use that prioritizes the well-being of society over individual gain?**

Epilogue: What's Next?

As we reach the end of this exploration of the future—one shaped by autonomous vehicles, humanoid robots, and the power of artificial intelligence —it's important to reflect on the journey we've embarked upon. The technologies discussed in these chapters are not simply tools that change the world around us; they reshape how we live, connect, and understand ourselves. But where do we go from here?

The road ahead is both exciting and uncertain. Technologies like self-driving cars and advanced robotics promise incredible gains in convenience, safety, and productivity. They also challenge us to rethink what work means, how we plan our cities, and how we distribute the benefits of progress fairly. The Age of Plenitude, with its promise of abundance, invites us to imagine a world where no one is left without the essentials, where AI and automation can free us to pursue creativity, personal growth, and community building.

Yet with all these promises come responsibilities. Ethical dilemmas must be addressed: ensuring that AI doesn't widen the gap between the rich and the underserved, that humanoid robots enhance rather than diminish our humanity, and that automation is used as a force for widespread prosperity, not control. The future is not written in code, but rather shaped by human hands, human choices, and human values. It is up to us to guide these technologies in ways that align with our highest ideals, promoting fairness, compassion, and sustainability.

To take an active role in shaping this future, we must start now. Engage with the AI tools available to you, educate yourself on the policies that will shape the world of tomorrow, and advocate for ethical practices within your communities and workplaces. Each small step we take today can lead to larger collective actions that will determine whether AI and automation serve the interests of all or only a few.

Ensuring that the benefits of AI and automation are shared equitably requires diverse voices and perspectives in shaping this future. It is crucial that individuals from all walks of life—across different regions, professions, and socioeconomic backgrounds—have a say in how these technologies evolve. By fostering inclusivity, we can build systems that serve humanity as a whole, rather than leaving anyone behind.

The future of technology is not bound by borders, and the challenges we face—like climate change, privacy concerns, and economic disparity—require global cooperation. It's through international collaboration that we can establish ethical standards, share resources, and ensure that advancements in AI, robotics, and automation benefit all of humanity, not just a select few. Working together, we can create a future where technology helps solve the world's most pressing problems.

The risks of inaction are real. Without careful guidance, these technologies could deepen inequalities, erode privacy, or concentrate power in the hands of a few. Failing to act now could leave us unprepared for the sweeping changes ahead, and risk leaving behind those who are already vulnerable. It is our shared responsibility to ensure that these advancements work for the good of all, rather than exacerbating existing divides.

As you imagine yourself in this future, whether it's cruising in an autonomous vehicle, co-working with a robot, or experiencing a world where scarcity is no longer the norm, remember that each of us has a role to play. Embrace lifelong learning, engage in dialogues about the technologies changing our lives, and think about how these advancements can be steered toward the common good. This is a future of our making—a collective effort that depends on our creativity, adaptability, and our commitment to ensuring that technology uplifts us all.

The future is coming, whether we are ready or not. Let's work to be ready together—not just as individuals, but as a connected, thoughtful community striving for a world where technology serves all of humanity, with fairness, compassion, and boundless possibility.

About the Author

J. Poole is a technology enthusiast and futurist with a deep commitment to exploring how emerging innovations can shape a better world. Passionate about making complex ideas accessible, he writes to inspire readers to think critically about the transformative role of technology in society. Through his work, J. encourages active participation in shaping a future where technology, ethics, and sustainability intersect.

A unique aspect of J. Poole's content creation process is his collaboration with AI technology. The stories and discussions presented on his YouTube channel, TechFrontiers, are brought to life through a combination of human creativity and advanced AI models. The AI-generated voices in the videos, coupled with Poole's insights, deliver thought-provoking content that covers a range of topics, including AI ethics, fusion energy, solar power, energy storage, and the future of energy infrastructure in an AGI-driven world.

By working alongside AI, J. Poole is able to blend cutting-edge technology with human intuition, creating engaging, high-quality content with seamless production efficiency. This partnership enables him to explore forward-thinking ideas and present them in a way that resonates with both tech enthusiasts and everyday readers, making complex technological advancements understandable and actionable for a wide audience.